A Guide for the Business Amateur

The Business Landscape

Roberts Follett

Introduction:

In the dynamic world of commerce, where opportunities abound but challenges lurk around every corner, the prospect of stepping into the realm of business can be both exhilarating and overwhelming, especially for those who identify as "business amateurs." This guide serves as a compass and companion for individuals at the outset of their entrepreneurial journey, offering a roadmap through the intricacies of the business landscape.

For the business amateur, this is more than a mere introduction; it is a portal to understanding the nuances of entrepreneurship, management, and strategic decision-making. In a realm often painted with jargon and complexities, this guide is designed to demystify the business world, providing clarity, insights, and actionable advice tailored to those taking their first steps into the expansive terrain of commerce.

As we embark on this journey together, we recognize that being a business amateur is not a limitation but a vantage point—a perspective that holds the potential for innovation, fresh perspectives, and untapped opportunities. This guide is crafted with the belief that every question, uncertainty, and challenge faced by the business amateur is an opportunity for growth, learning, and the development of a resilient entrepreneurial spirit.

From foundational concepts to practical tips, "Navigating the Business Landscape" seeks to empower business amateurs with the knowledge and confidence needed to navigate the intricacies of the corporate world. Whether you're a recent graduate, a budding entrepreneur, or someone contemplating a career shift, this guide is tailored to meet you where you are and accompany you on your journey towards understanding, mastering, and thriving in the multifaceted world of business.

So, let the exploration begin—a journey of discovery, learning, and empowerment for the business amateur ready to transform curiosity into competence, uncertainty into strategy, and passion into tangible success. Welcome to a guide that goes beyond the basics, inviting you to not only navigate the business landscape but to chart your own course towards success.

Table of Contents

Introduction

Chapter One

1.1 About the Guide

In the vast expanse of the business landscape, the journey of the business amateur is both exhilarating and challenging. This section aims to provide a comprehensive understanding of the guide's purpose, its intended audience, and the roadmap it offers to those venturing into the dynamic world of business.

The Purpose of the Guide: Nurturing Growth and Understanding

At the core of this guide lies a fundamental objective – to serve as a beacon for individuals setting foot into the intricate tapestry of business. More than a manual, this guide is a companion, offering insights, wisdom, and practical advice curated to foster growth and understanding.

In a world where business concepts can often seem daunting and impenetrable, the guide takes on the responsibility of demystifying complexities. It acts as a mentor, providing clarity on the fundamental principles that govern the business terrain. Whether you are a recent graduate, a budding entrepreneur, or someone navigating a career shift, this guide is tailored to meet you at your starting point, acknowledging the unique challenges and opportunities that come with being a business amateur.

Who Should Embark on This Journey?

This guide is designed for the curious minds, the ambitious souls, and the relentless dreamers who are ready to embark on a journey of self-discovery within the realms of business. If you find yourself intrigued by the dynamics of commerce, eager to understand the intricacies of entrepreneurship, or simply seeking a roadmap for success in the business world, you are the ideal reader for this guide.

- Recent Graduates: For those fresh out of academia, entering the business world can be a formidable transition. This guide serves as a bridge, helping graduates navigate the shift from theory to practical application, equipping them with the tools needed for a successful transition.

- Budding Entrepreneurs: If you harbor aspirations of launching your venture, this guide provides invaluable insights into the entrepreneurial mindset, identifying opportunities, and overcoming the challenges inherent in building and scaling a business.

- Career Shifters: Individuals contemplating a shift in their professional journey will find this guide to be a strategic companion. Whether moving from one industry to another or embracing entrepreneurship after years in the corporate world, the guide offers guidance tailored to the unique challenges of such transitions.

What Sets This Guide Apart?

Beyond being a mere compilation of business principles, this guide distinguishes itself through its holistic approach. It recognizes that the business amateur is not confined to a single archetype but represents a diverse community with varying backgrounds, aspirations, and levels of experience.

- Practical Insights: Each chapter is crafted to provide not only theoretical knowledge but also practical insights. Real-world examples, case studies, and actionable tips permeate the guide, ensuring that the reader gains a hands-on understanding of the concepts discussed.

- Navigational Framework: The guide is structured as a roadmap, guiding the reader through the sequential aspects of understanding the business landscape, delving into entrepreneurship, mastering business management, overcoming challenges, and ultimately crafting a personalized journey toward success.

How to Navigate the Guide:

To maximize the benefit derived from this guide, readers are encouraged to explore the chapters sequentially, allowing for a natural progression of knowledge acquisition. However, each chapter is designed to be self-contained, enabling readers to dive into specific topics of interest based on their immediate needs.

- Icons and Callouts: Throughout the guide, icons and callouts will highlight key concepts, actionable steps, and noteworthy insights. These visual cues are intended to enhance engagement and facilitate a quick grasp of essential information.

- Interactive Elements: Look out for interactive elements, including exercises, reflection prompts, and links to additional resources. These elements are strategically integrated to encourage active participation and facilitate a deeper understanding of the concepts discussed.

As we embark on this journey together, Section 1.1 serves as a prelude—a stage-setting introduction to a guide crafted with meticulous care and consideration for the unique needs of the business amateur. It is an invitation to explore, learn, and transform curiosity into competence, uncertainty into strategy, and passion into tangible success. With this guide, the business landscape becomes not just a terrain to navigate but a canvas upon which the business amateur can craft their narrative of achievement.

Continue the exploration by delving into subsequent sections to uncover the rich tapestry of insights and guidance tailored to your journey as a business amateur.

1.2 The Significance of Being a Business Amateur

Embracing the Identity: Beyond Inexperience

In the realm of business, the term "amateur" is often mistakenly equated with inexperience or inadequacy. However, this section aims to redefine the narrative, emphasizing the significance of being a business amateur as a unique and valuable perspective.

The Business Amateur Advantage: A Fresh Lens on Innovation

Being a business amateur is not a deficit; it's an asset. The fresh perspective unburdened by preconceived notions or industry dogmas provides a unique lens through which to view the business landscape. The absence of deep-rooted habits allows for a malleability that can be a catalyst for innovation.

- Unconventional Thinking: The business amateur, unencumbered by industry norms, is more likely to entertain unconventional ideas and approaches. This section explores how this freedom from pre-established frameworks can lead to groundbreaking solutions and the cultivation of a culture of innovation.

- Adaptability as a Strength: The business landscape is dynamic, with constant changes in technology, market trends, and consumer behavior. Business amateurs, by virtue of their adaptability, can navigate these changes more fluidly. This section delves into how the ability to adapt becomes a powerful tool in the arsenal of a business amateur.

Learning as an Ongoing Process: The Growth Mindset

One of the key attributes of a successful business amateur is the commitment to continuous learning. This section explores the concept of a growth mindset and how it propels individuals from a state of inexperience to one of perpetual growth.

- Cultivating Curiosity. Curiosity is the fuel that propels the journey of a business amateur. By fostering a sense of wonder and a desire to understand, business amateurs can transform challenges into learning opportunities. The section discusses practical ways to cultivate curiosity in the pursuit of knowledge.

- Resilience in the Face of Challenges: In the unpredictable terrain of business, challenges are inevitable. The business amateur, armed with a growth mindset, approaches challenges as stepping stones rather than obstacles. This section explores resilience as a key component of the growth mindset and its role in shaping success.

 Building a Unique Skill Set: The Power of Diverse Experiences

While seasoned professionals may possess deep expertise in a specific domain, business amateurs bring a diverse skill set shaped by varied experiences. This section delves into how the amalgamation of skills from different fields can be a potent asset in navigating the complex business landscape.

- Transferable Skills: The skills acquired in one context can often be transferred to another, providing business amateurs with a toolkit that goes beyond the confines of a single industry. This section highlights the value of transferable skills and how they contribute to the adaptability of business amateurs.

- Interdisciplinary Insights: Drawing insights from various disciplines fosters a holistic understanding of business challenges. Business amateurs, unbound by siloed knowledge, can bring interdisciplinary perspectives to problem-solving. The section explores how this interdisciplinary approach can lead to innovative solutions.

Networking and Collaboration: Leveraging the Collective Wisdom

While experience is often associated with an individual's journey, the significance of networking and collaboration in the business world cannot be overstated. Business amateurs, by virtue of their position, have the opportunity to forge connections and tap into collective wisdom.

- Building a Support Network: Establishing connections with mentors, peers, and industry experts is a strategic move for business amateurs. This section discusses the importance of mentorship and networking in accelerating the learning curve and gaining insights from those who have navigated similar paths.

- Collaborative Innovation: Business is increasingly becoming a collaborative endeavor. By fostering a collaborative mindset, business amateurs can tap into diverse perspectives and skill sets. The section explores how collaboration can be a catalyst for innovation and business growth.
This section concludes by emphasizing the inherent potential of business amateurs to contribute fresh ideas, adapt to change, foster a growth mindset, and build a unique skill set. It sets the stage for the journey ahead, where the business amateur is not merely a learner but a catalyst for positive transformation in the business landscape.

1.3 Navigating the Business Landscape: A Brief Overview

Unveiling the Vast Terrain of Business

This section provides a panoramic overview of the business landscape, setting the stage for the business amateur to comprehend the multifaceted dimensions they are about to explore. It introduces the key components of the business environment, the stakeholders involved, and the ever-evolving dynamics that shape the entrepreneurial journey.

The Ecosystem of Business: Understanding the Dynamics

- Market Forces and Trends: Business is not a static entity; it is a living, breathing ecosystem influenced by market forces and trends. This subsection explores the dynamic nature of markets, the forces that drive change, and the importance of staying attuned to trends for strategic decision-making.

- Regulatory Frameworks: Navigating the legal and regulatory landscape is crucial for any business. This subsection provides an overview of the regulatory frameworks that businesses must navigate, emphasizing the importance of compliance and ethical conduct.

Key Players in the Business Landscape: Understanding Stakeholders

- Customers: At the heart of any business are its customers. Understanding their needs, preferences, and behaviors is essential for success. This subsection delves into customer-centric approaches and the significance of building strong customer relationships.

- Competitors: In a competitive landscape, knowledge about competitors is a strategic advantage. This subsection discusses the importance of competitor analysis and how businesses can leverage insights to position themselves effectively.

- Suppliers and Partnerships: The relationships a business forms with suppliers and partners can significantly impact its operations. This subsection explores the dynamics of supplier relationships and the strategic importance of forming fruitful partnerships.

Economic Forces: The Macroscopic Influences on Business

- Economic Indicators: Business is intricately linked to the broader economy. This subsection explores key economic indicators, such as GDP, inflation, and unemployment, and how businesses can interpret these factors to make informed decisions.

- Globalization and International Business: In an interconnected world, businesses are increasingly engaging in international markets. This subsection discusses the opportunities and challenges of globalization and how businesses can navigate the complexities of international trade.

Strategic Business Management: The Art of Decision-Making

- Strategic Planning: Formulating a clear and effective strategy is paramount for business success. This subsection explores the strategic planning process, including goal setting, SWOT analysis, and the development of action plans.

- Leadership and Management Styles: The effectiveness of leadership and management styles can shape the culture of a business. This subsection delves into different leadership styles and management approaches, emphasizing their impact on organizational success.

Technology and Innovation: Catalysts for Business Transformation

- Technological Advancements: In the digital age, technology is a driving force behind business innovation. This subsection explores the role of technology in business, from automation to artificial intelligence, and how businesses can leverage these advancements.

- Innovation Culture: Fostering a culture of innovation is essential for businesses seeking to stay ahead in a rapidly changing landscape. This subsection discusses strategies for creating an innovation-friendly environment within organizations.

As we conclude this overview, the business landscape reveals itself as a vast and dynamic terrain, rich with opportunities and challenges. Section 1.3 serves as a compass, orienting the business amateur to the key components of the landscape they are about to navigate. Armed with this foundational knowledge, the business amateur is ready to embark on a journey of discovery and mastery, exploring the diverse facets of entrepreneurship, management, and strategic decision-making in the chapters that follow.

Chapter Two:
Understanding the Business Terrain

Introduction:

As we transition from the foundational concepts laid out in the initial chapter, the journey of the business amateur advances into Chapter Two—a critical juncture that delves deep into the core of the business landscape. This chapter serves as a comprehensive exploration of the various components that shape the terrain of commerce. It is not merely a theoretical exploration but a practical guide designed to equip business amateurs with a nuanced understanding of the dynamic forces that influence the business environment.

2.1 The Dynamics of Modern Commerce

Unraveling the Complexity:

In the intricate web of modern commerce, understanding the dynamics that govern the business environment is paramount for success. Section 2.1 serves as a gateway into this expansive realm, shedding light on the multifaceted forces that businesses must navigate.

The Evolving Nature of Markets:

Commerce is a living, breathing entity, subject to constant evolution. Markets are not static; they ebb and flow, responding to economic, social, and technological shifts. Business amateurs must grasp the concept of market dynamics, recognizing that what worked yesterday may not necessarily work tomorrow.

- Market Trends and Consumer Behavior: This subsection delves into the importance of staying abreast of market trends and understanding consumer behavior. By interpreting these dynamics, business amateurs can identify opportunities, anticipate changes, and tailor their strategies to meet evolving demands.

- Globalization's Impact: The global interconnectedness of markets is an undeniable reality. This subsection explores how globalization influences markets, providing both opportunities for expansion and challenges in adapting to diverse cultural and economic contexts.

Technology as a Catalyst:

In the contemporary business landscape, technology stands as a powerful catalyst for change. This subsection examines the transformative impact of technology on commerce, from the rise of e-commerce to the integration of artificial intelligence.

- Digital Transformation: Businesses are undergoing a digital revolution, reshaping traditional processes and customer interactions. This subsection outlines the essentials of digital transformation and how businesses can leverage technology to enhance efficiency and innovation.

- Adapting to Technological Advances: The pace of technological change can be overwhelming. This subsection provides guidance on how business amateurs can navigate this landscape, emphasizing the importance of agility and a proactive approach to technology adoption.

Adapting to Change:

The business terrain is inherently volatile, requiring businesses to be agile and adaptive. Section 2.1 underscores the significance of embracing change as a constant, recognizing that businesses must evolve alongside the dynamic forces that shape the marketplace.

2.2 Key Players and Stakeholders

Mapping the Business Ecosystem:

In the intricate dance of commerce, businesses do not operate in isolation. They are integral components of a broader ecosystem, and understanding the roles played by key players and stakeholders is fundamental for effective navigation.

The Central Role of Customers:

Customers are the lifeblood of any business. This subsection explores the pivotal role customers play in the success of a business, emphasizing the need for customer-centric approaches in product development, marketing, and overall business strategy.

- Customer Relationship Management (CRM): Building and maintaining strong relationships with customers is a strategic imperative. This subsection delves into CRM strategies, emphasizing personalized interactions, feedback mechanisms, and the cultivation of customer loyalty.

- The Power of Customer Feedback: In an age of connectivity, customer feedback is more accessible and influential than ever. This subsection explores how businesses can harness the power of customer feedback to refine products, enhance services, and foster a customer-centric culture.

The Chessboard of Competition:

Competition is inherent in the business landscape, and recognizing the dynamics of competitive forces is vital. This subsection explores the concept of competitive analysis, guiding business amateurs in understanding competitors, differentiating their offerings, and positioning themselves strategically.

- SWOT Analysis: A fundamental tool in strategic planning, SWOT analysis allows businesses to assess their Strengths, Weaknesses, Opportunities, and Threats. This subsection provides a step-by-step guide on how to conduct a SWOT analysis and leverage the insights gained.

- Strategic Positioning: Beyond understanding competitors, businesses must strategically position themselves in the market. This subsection delves into the art of strategic positioning, exploring concepts such as differentiation, niche targeting, and creating a unique value proposition.

The Collaborative Web:

Businesses do not operate in isolation but within a network of relationships and collaborations. This subsection illuminates the significance of building strong relationships with suppliers, forging partnerships, and engaging in collaborations to enhance overall business efficacy.

- Supplier Relationships: Reliable and efficient supply chains are the backbone of many businesses. This subsection explores strategies for building and maintaining strong relationships with suppliers, ensuring a seamless flow of goods and services.

- Strategic Partnerships: Collaborative ventures can unlock new opportunities. This subsection examines the strategic considerations behind forming partnerships, whether for joint ventures, co-marketing initiatives, or alliances that amplify mutual strengths.

The Societal Impact:

Businesses, as integral members of society, wield significant influence. Section 2.2 extends the exploration beyond immediate business relationships to consider the broader impact of commerce on communities, ethical considerations, and corporate social responsibility.

2.3 Economic Forces at Play

The Macroscopic View:

Beyond the microcosm of individual businesses, the economic forces that shape the broader landscape have profound implications. Section 2.3

zooms out to explore the macroeconomic factors that influence business operations, strategic decision-making, and long-term sustainability.

 Economic Indicators:

Economic indicators serve as barometers, providing insights into the health and trajectory of economies. This subsection introduces key economic indicators, such as Gross Domestic Product (GDP), inflation rates, and unemployment figures, decoding their significance for businesses.

- Interpreting GDP: GDP is a fundamental measure of economic health. This subsection delves into the nuances of GDP, discussing how businesses can interpret GDP data to gauge the overall economic climate and make informed decisions.

- Inflation and Its Impact: Inflation rates influence pricing strategies, consumer purchasing power, and overall economic stability. This subsection explores the impact of inflation on businesses and strategies for mitigating its effects.

Globalization and International Business:

In an era of increased interconnectedness, businesses are not confined by national borders. This subsection examines the opportunities and challenges presented by globalization, providing insights into international trade, cultural considerations, and strategies for global market entry.

- Expanding Horizons: Businesses eyeing international markets must navigate diverse landscapes. This subsection offers guidance on the intricacies of international expansion, from understanding cultural nuances to overcoming logistical challenges.

- Risk Management in Global Operations: Operating in diverse regions introduces new risks. This subsection explores strategies for effective risk management in global operations, including currency risks, geopolitical considerations, and cultural sensitivities.

Strategic Decision-Making in an Economic Context:

Understanding economic forces is foundational to strategic decision-making. Section 2.3 culminates with an exploration of how businesses can align their strategies with the prevailing economic climate, ensuring resilience and sustainability.

As we conclude this comprehensive exploration of Chapter Two, the business amateur emerges with a deepened understanding of the intricacies that define the business landscape. From the dynamic forces shaping markets to the intricate web of relationships with stakeholders, and the macroeconomic factors influencing strategic decisions—Chapter Two lays a robust foundation for the journey ahead.

In the subsequent chapters, we will continue to build upon this foundation, delving into the essentials of entrepreneurship the principles of effective business management, and the art of strategic decision-making. The business landscape, once perceived as a complex and daunting terrain, now unfolds as a realm of opportunities waiting to be harnessed by the informed and strategic business amateur.

Chapter Three
Foundations of Entrepreneurship

Introduction:

Chapter Three marks a pivotal juncture in the journey of the business amateur. As we transition from understanding the dynamic forces of the business landscape, we delve into the very essence of entrepreneurial spirit—the foundations of entrepreneurship. This chapter serves as a compass, guiding business amateurs through the fundamental principles that underpin successful ventures, exploring the mindset, strategies, and practicalities that define the world of entrepreneurship.

3.1 Defining Entrepreneurship

Unveiling the Entrepreneurial Mindset:

At the heart of every successful venture lies the entrepreneurial mindset—a unique blend of vision, resilience, and innovation. Section 3.1 unravels the intricacies of entrepreneurship, offering insights into what defines an entrepreneur and the key attributes that set them apart.

The Essence of Entrepreneurship:

Entrepreneurship is not merely a profession; it's a mindset, a way of thinking that thrives on challenges and sees opportunities where others see obstacles. This subsection delves into the essence of entrepreneurship, exploring the passion, risk-taking, and determination that characterize the entrepreneurial spirit.

- Passion as the Driving Force: At the core of entrepreneurship is a deep-seated passion. This subsection explores how passion fuels the entrepreneurial journey, driving individuals to overcome obstacles, persist in the face of challenges, and stay committed to their vision.

- Embracing Risk and Uncertainty: Entrepreneurship is inherently linked to risk. This subsection examines the relationship between entrepreneurship and risk, exploring the calculated risks entrepreneurs take, the fear of failure, and the resilience required to navigate uncertainty.

The Entrepreneurial Mindset:

The mindset of an entrepreneur distinguishes them in a crowded business landscape. This subsection dissects the components of the entrepreneurial mindset, from a relentless pursuit of goals to a willingness to learn and adapt in the face of evolving challenges.

- Vision and Goal Setting: Entrepreneurs are driven by a clear vision of what they want to achieve. This subsection explores the importance of vision and goal setting, providing practical strategies for business amateurs to define their aspirations and map out their entrepreneurial journey.

- Adaptability and Continuous Learning: The business landscape is dynamic, and successful entrepreneurs embrace change. This subsection discusses the significance of adaptability and continuous learning, illustrating how these qualities foster resilience and agility.

Entrepreneurial Archetypes:

Entrepreneurs come in various forms, each with its unique strengths and characteristics. This subsection introduces different entrepreneurial archetypes, from the visionary founder to the social entrepreneur, offering business amateurs a glimpse into the diverse paths they can traverse.

- Innovators and Visionaries: Some entrepreneurs are driven by a vision to innovate and create. This subsection explores the mindset of innovators and visionaries, shedding light on how they bring groundbreaking ideas to fruition and shape industries.

- Social Entrepreneurs: Beyond profits, some entrepreneurs are dedicated to creating positive social impact. This subsection delves into the world of social entrepreneurship, examining how businesses can be a force for good while still achieving financial success.

The Entrepreneurial Journey:

Understanding entrepreneurship is not complete without an exploration of the entrepreneurial journey. Section 3.1 concludes by providing a roadmap for the business amateur, outlining the stages of entrepreneurship from ideation to scaling and offering insights into the challenges and triumphs that characterize this dynamic journey.

3.2 Identifying Opportunities

The Art of Opportunity Recognition:

Opportunity recognition is the lifeblood of entrepreneurship. Section 3.2 delves into the intricate process of identifying opportunities, guiding business amateurs in honing their skills to spot potential ventures, innovate, and transform ideas into actionable plans.

Developing a Keen Observational Eye:

Opportunities often disguise themselves as challenges, trends, or unmet needs. This subsection emphasizes the importance of keen observation, encouraging business amateurs to cultivate an acute awareness of their surroundings, industries of interest, and emerging trends.

- Market Gaps and Unmet Needs: Successful entrepreneurs excel at identifying gaps in the market and unmet needs. This subsection explores how business amateurs can leverage their observational skills to uncover opportunities and create solutions that resonate with consumers.

- Trends and Industry Shifts: Industries are dynamic, undergoing constant shifts. This subsection discusses the significance of staying attuned to trends and industry changes, showcasing how business amateurs can position themselves to capitalize on emerging opportunities.

Idea Generation and Innovation:

In the realm of entrepreneurship, ideas are the currency of innovation. This subsection unravels the art of idea generation, exploring techniques for sparking creativity, fostering innovation, and transforming raw concepts into viable business propositions.

- Brainstorming Techniques: Creativity is a skill that can be cultivated. This subsection introduces various brainstorming techniques, from traditional methods to collaborative ideation sessions, empowering business amateurs to generate a diverse range of ideas.

- Innovation as a Competitive Advantage: In a competitive landscape, innovation sets businesses apart. This subsection discusses the role of innovation as a competitive advantage, showcasing how entrepreneurs can

infuse creativity into their ventures to stay ahead.

Market Research and Validation:

An idea's potential hinges on its alignment with market needs. This subsection delves into the importance of market research and validation, offering practical insights into conducting thorough assessments to ensure that identified opportunities have real-world demand.

- Understanding Target Audiences: Successful entrepreneurs understand their target audiences intimately. This subsection explores strategies for defining and understanding target audiences, allowing business amateurs to tailor their products or services to specific market segments.

- Prototype Testing and Feedback: Before a full-scale launch, testing prototypes and seeking feedback are crucial steps. This subsection guides business amateurs in designing effective testing methodologies, collecting valuable feedback, and refining their offerings based on insights gained.

Evaluating Risk and Return:

Opportunity identification is inherently linked to risk evaluation. Section 3.2 concludes by examining the delicate balance between risk and return, providing business amateurs with frameworks for assessing potential ventures and making informed decisions.

3.3 The Entrepreneurial Mindset

Cultivating the Seeds of Entrepreneurial Thinking:

The entrepreneurial mindset is not a fixed trait but a dynamic quality that can be nurtured and developed. Section 3.3 delves into the core principles of the entrepreneurial mindset, offering business amateurs a blueprint for cultivating the mental resilience, adaptability, and creativity that define successful entrepreneurs.

Embracing Failure as a Stepping Stone:

Failure is an integral part of the entrepreneurial journey. This subsection explores the concept of embracing failure not as a roadblock but as a stepping stone toward growth and learning, reframing setbacks as opportunities for refinement and improvement.

- Resilience in the Face of Setbacks: Resilience is the cornerstone of the entrepreneurial mindset. This subsection delves into the importance of cultivating resilience, providing strategies for bouncing back from failures, adapting to challenges, and persisting in the pursuit of goals.

- Learning from Mistakes: Every mistake is an invaluable lesson. This subsection discusses the art of learning from mistakes, encouraging business amateurs to approach challenges with a growth mindset and view setbacks as opportunities for self-improvement.

Decisiveness and Action Orientation:

In the fast-paced world of entrepreneurship, decisiveness is a prized trait. This subsection explores the importance of making timely decisions, taking calculated risks, and maintaining an action-oriented approach to transform ideas into tangible outcomes.

- Overcoming Decision Paralysis: Decision-making can be daunting, especially in the face of uncertainty. This subsection provides practical strategies for overcoming decision paralysis, empowering business amateurs to make informed and timely choices.

- Iterative Action and Adaptation: The entrepreneurial journey is marked by continuous iteration. This subsection discusses the iterative nature of entrepreneurship, emphasizing the importance of taking initial actions, gathering feedback, and adapting strategies accordingly.

Fostering Creativity and Innovation:

Creativity is the fuel that propels entrepreneurial ventures forward. This subsection explores techniques for fostering creativity, from adopting a curious mindset to engaging in activities that stimulate innovation and nurture a culture of continuous ideation.

- Curiosity as a Catalyst: Curiosity is the spark that ignites creativity. This subsection delves into the role of curiosity in entrepreneurial thinking, encouraging business amateurs to ask questions, seek new perspectives, and explore uncharted territories.

- Creating an Innovation-Friendly Environment: Innovation flourishes in environments that encourage experimentation and collaboration. This subsection provides insights into creating an innovation-friendly culture within entrepreneurial ventures, fostering a mindset that thrives on creative problem-solving.

The Lifelong Journey of Entrepreneurial Mindset Development:

As Section 3.3 concludes, it sets the stage for business amateurs to embark on a lifelong journey of entrepreneurial mindset development. The entrepreneurial mindset is not a destination but a continuous process of growth, adaptation, and transformation—a journey that defines the very essence of successful entrepreneurship.

Chapter Three unfolds as a launchpad, propelling business amateurs into the heart of entrepreneurship. From defining the entrepreneurial mindset to identifying opportunities and cultivating the mental resilience needed for the journey ahead, this chapter equips aspiring entrepreneurs with the foundational principles that pave the way for success. As we move forward, the entrepreneurial spirit becomes not just a concept to grasp but a force to be harnessed, propelling business amateurs toward a future of innovation, growth, and accomplishment.

Chapter Four:
Essentials of Business Management

Introduction:

As we progress in the journey of the business amateur, Chapter Four emerges as a cornerstone—a comprehensive exploration of the essentials of business management. This chapter delves into the principles and practices that form the bedrock of effective business operations. From organizational leadership to strategic decision-making, Chapter Four is a roadmap for business amateurs to not only navigate but thrive in the complex terrain of managing and leading successful enterprises.

4.1 Principles of Effective Management

The Art and Science of Management:

Effective management is both an art and a science, requiring a delicate balance of strategic thinking, interpersonal skills, and operational acumen. Section 4.1 serves as a gateway into the principles that underpin successful business management, providing business amateurs with the foundational knowledge to steer organizations toward success.

The Role of Leadership:

Leadership is the keystone of effective management. This subsection explores the multifaceted role of leadership in guiding organizations, fostering a positive organizational culture, and inspiring teams to achieve their full potential.

- Leadership Styles and Their Impact: Different situations call for different leadership styles. This subsection delves into various leadership styles, from authoritative to transformational, discussing their characteristics, advantages, and potential applications in different organizational contexts.

- The Visionary Leader: Visionary leaders have the ability to inspire and guide teams toward a shared vision. This subsection explores the traits of visionary leadership, emphasizing the importance of a compelling vision in rallying teams and driving organizational success.

Organizational Culture and Climate:

The culture of an organization shapes its identity, influences employee behavior, and impacts overall performance. This subsection examines the concept of organizational culture, exploring how business amateurs can cultivate a positive climate that aligns with their values and goals.

- Creating a Positive Work Environment: A positive work environment is conducive to employee satisfaction and productivity. This subsection provides strategies for creating a positive workplace culture, from fostering open communication to recognizing and celebrating achievements.

- Diversity and Inclusion: Embracing diversity and fostering inclusion are integral to a vibrant organizational culture. This subsection discusses the importance of diversity in the workplace, offering insights into creating an inclusive environment that values diverse perspectives and backgrounds.

Effective Communication:

Communication is the lifeblood of successful management. This subsection delves into the nuances of effective communication, from articulating a compelling vision to fostering transparent and open dialogue within the organization.

- Strategies for Clear Communication: Clear communication is essential for avoiding misunderstandings and aligning teams. This subsection explores practical strategies for enhancing communication, from active listening to utilizing appropriate channels for different types of messages.

- Feedback and Performance Communication: Regular feedback is instrumental in employee development. This subsection provides insights into delivering constructive feedback, conducting performance reviews, and fostering a culture of continuous improvement.

Strategic Decision-Making

The Decision-Making Process:

Effective management hinges on sound decision-making. This subsection unravels the decision-making process, providing business amateurs with a framework for analyzing options, mitigating risks, and making informed decisions that align with organizational goals.

- SWOT Analysis Revisited: SWOT analysis is a powerful tool for strategic decision-making. This subsection revisits the concept, showcasing how business amateurs can apply SWOT analysis to evaluate internal strengths and weaknesses, as well as external opportunities and threats.

- Decision Trees and Scenario Analysis: Complex decisions often benefit from visualizing different scenarios. This subsection introduces decision trees and scenario analysis as decision-making tools, offering insights into how these methods can help assess potential outcomes and inform strategic choices.

Risk Management:

In the dynamic landscape of business, risks are inevitable. This subsection explores the principles of risk management, guiding business amateurs in identifying, assessing, and mitigating risks to safeguard organizational interests.

- Risk Identification and Assessment: Proactive risk management begins with identifying potential risks. This subsection discusses strategies for systematically identifying and assessing risks, from market fluctuations to operational challenges.

- Risk Mitigation Strategies: Once risks are identified, effective mitigation strategies are crucial. This subsection provides a toolkit of risk mitigation strategies, including contingency planning, insurance, and strategic partnerships, empowering business amateurs to navigate uncertainties with resilience.

Strategic Planning and Goal Setting:

Strategic planning is the compass that guides organizations toward their desired future. This subsection explores the principles of strategic planning, emphasizing the importance of setting clear goals, formulating actionable strategies, and aligning organizational efforts with a long-term vision.

- SMART Goals: Setting SMART (Specific, Measurable, Achievable, Relevant, Time-Bound) goals is a fundamental aspect of strategic planning. This subsection provides practical guidelines for formulating SMART goals that drive organizational success.

- Developing Actionable Strategies: Goals are meaningless without actionable strategies. This subsection delves into the process of developing effective strategies that translate organizational objectives into tangible steps, fostering a roadmap for success.

Operational Efficiency and Continuous Improvement

Maximizing Operational Efficiency:

Efficient operations are the backbone of successful organizations. This subsection explores the principles of operational efficiency, guiding business amateurs in optimizing processes, managing resources effectively, and enhancing overall organizational performance.

- Lean Management Principles: Lean management focuses on eliminating waste and maximizing value. This subsection introduces the principles of lean management, showcasing how organizations can streamline processes to improve efficiency and deliver greater value to customers.

- Supply Chain Optimization: A well-optimized supply chain is essential for operational excellence.

This subsection discusses strategies for optimizing supply chain management, from demand forecasting to inventory management, ensuring a seamless flow of goods and services.

Continuous Improvement and Innovation:

The journey of effective management is an iterative one. This subsection explores the concept of continuous improvement, emphasizing the importance of fostering a culture that encourages innovation, learning from experiences, and evolving in response to changing circumstances.

- Kaizen and Continuous Improvement Models: Kaizen, a Japanese term for continuous improvement, is a guiding principle for organizational growth. This subsection introduces Kaizen and other continuous improvement models, illustrating how organizations can implement these principles to enhance performance.

- Encouraging a Culture of Innovation: Innovation is the engine that drives organizational evolution. This subsection provides insights into creating a culture that fosters innovation, encouraging employees to contribute ideas, experiment with new approaches, and embrace change.

Human Resource Management

Talent Acquisition and Development:

The success of any organization hinges on its people. This subsection explores the principles of human resource management, guiding business amateurs in talent acquisition, employee development, and creating a positive and inclusive workplace.

- Recruitment Strategies: Acquiring the right talent is a strategic advantage. This subsection delves into recruitment strategies, from leveraging digital platforms to conducting effective interviews, ensuring organizations attract and retain skilled professionals.

- Employee Training and Development: Investing in employee development pays long-term dividends. This subsection discusses strategies for designing effective training programs, fostering a culture of continuous learning, and nurturing the professional growth of employees.

Employee Engagement and Motivation:

Engaged and motivated employees are the driving force behind organizational success. This subsection explores the principles of employee engagement and motivation, offering practical insights into fostering a workplace culture that inspires commitment and enthusiasm.

- Recognition and Rewards: Recognizing and rewarding employees for their contributions is a cornerstone of motivation. This subsection provides strategies for implementing effective recognition and reward programs, boosting morale and reinforcing positive behaviors.

- Employee Feedback and Surveys: Regular feedback mechanisms are vital for understanding employee sentiments. This subsection discusses the importance of feedback and surveys, offering guidance on how organizations can solicit and utilize employee input to enhance workplace satisfaction.

Financial Management and Sustainability

Financial Planning and Budgeting:

Sound financial management is the linchpin of organizational sustainability. This subsection explores the principles of financial planning and budgeting, guiding business amateurs in allocating resources efficiently, managing cash flow, and ensuring fiscal responsibility.

- Budget Development and Monitoring: Developing a comprehensive budget is essential for financial stability. This subsection provides practical steps for budget development and monitoring, helping organizations align financial resources with strategic priorities.

- Cash Flow Management: Cash flow is the lifeblood of businesses. This subsection discusses strategies for effective cash flow management, from optimizing invoicing processes to managing accounts payable and receivable, ensuring financial resilience.

 Sustainability and Corporate Social Responsibility (CSR):

Organizational success is increasingly linked to sustainability and social responsibility. This subsection explores the principles of sustainability and CSR, guiding business amateurs in incorporating ethical practices, environmental considerations, and social impact into their operations.

- Environmental Sustainability: Adopting environmentally sustainable practices is not just a moral imperative but a strategic necessity. This subsection discusses how organizations can embrace eco-friendly initiatives, reduce their carbon footprint, and contribute to environmental conservation.

- Social Impact and Community Engagement: Corporate social responsibility extends beyond profit margins. This subsection provides insights into how organizations can engage with communities, support social causes, and contribute to the well-being of society at large.

Crisis Management and Adaptability

Preparing for and Managing Crises:

Crisis is an inevitable part of organizational life. This subsection explores the principles of crisis management, providing business amateurs with strategies for anticipating, preparing for, and effectively managing crises to minimize disruptions.

- Risk Assessment and Scenario Planning: Proactive risk assessment is crucial for crisis preparedness. This subsection discusses the importance of risk assessment and scenario planning, equipping organizations to anticipate potential crises and develop response strategies.

- Communication Strategies in Crisis: Effective communication is paramount during crises. This subsection provides guidance on developing communication strategies that maintain transparency, address concerns, and uphold organizational credibility in challenging times.

Adaptability and Change Management:

In the fast-paced business landscape, adaptability is a competitive advantage. This subsection explores the principles of change management, offering insights into how organizations can foster adaptability, embrace change, and position themselves for sustained success.

- Change Readiness: Organizations must be prepared to embrace change. This subsection discusses strategies for cultivating a culture of change readiness, empowering employees to adapt to new circumstances and contribute to organizational resilience.

- Agile Management Principles: Agile management principles provide a framework for adapting to change swiftly and efficiently. This subsection introduces agile principles, illustrating how organizations can apply these principles to enhance flexibility and responsiveness.

Ethical Leadership and Corporate Governance

Upholding Ethical Standards:

Ethical leadership is the bedrock of organizational integrity. This subsection explores the principles of ethical leadership, emphasizing the importance of upholding ethical standards, promoting transparency, and fostering a culture of integrity within organizations.

- Ethical Decision-Making: Ethical decision-making requires a principled approach. This subsection provides a framework for ethical decision-making, helping leaders navigate complex situations while upholding values and principles.

- Whistleblowing and Reporting Mechanisms: Creating avenues for reporting ethical concerns is essential. This subsection discusses the importance of whistleblowing mechanisms, providing guidance on establishing effective reporting channels that encourage transparency and accountability.

Corporate Governance Practices:

Effective corporate governance ensures organizational accountability and sustainability. This subsection explores the principles of corporate governance, guiding business amateurs in establishing robust governance structures, accountability mechanisms, and ethical frameworks.

- Board Oversight and Accountability: Boards play a crucial role in governance. This subsection discusses the responsibilities of boards in providing oversight, ensuring accountability, and aligning organizational actions with stakeholder interests.

- Stakeholder Engagement: Engaging with stakeholders is central to good governance. This subsection provides insights into stakeholder engagement strategies, emphasizing the importance of open communication, transparency, and addressing stakeholder concerns.

Chapter Four unfolds as a comprehensive toolkit, equipping business amateurs with the essential principles and practices of effective business management. From leadership and strategic decision-making to operational efficiency, human resource management, financial sustainability, crisis management, and ethical leadership, this chapter provides a holistic understanding of the intricacies involved in steering organizations toward success.

As we proceed in the journey, the business amateur is not just a spectator of the business landscape but an active participant, armed with the knowledge and skills needed to navigate challenges, foster innovation, and lead organizations toward sustained excellence. Chapter Four sets the stage for business management mastery—an essential element in the arsenal of the aspiring business professional.

4.2 Building Effective Teams

The success of any organization hinges not only on individual competencies but also on the collective strength of its teams. Section 4.2 delves into the art and science of building effective teams, offering business amateurs insights into team dynamics, collaboration strategies, and leadership principles that foster a culture of innovation and high performance.

Understanding Team Dynamics:

Building effective teams starts with a deep understanding of team dynamics. Teams are not just collections of individuals but intricate ecosystems where collaboration, communication, and shared goals intersect. This subsection explores the foundational principles of team dynamics, providing business amateurs with the knowledge needed to cultivate environments where teams thrive.

- Forming, Storming, Norming, Performing: Tuckman's stages of group development—forming, storming, norming, and performing—offer a framework for understanding team dynamics. This subsection delves into each stage, illustrating how teams evolve, establish norms, and reach peak performance.

- Role Allocation and Synergy: Every team member plays a unique role in contributing to the team's success. This subsection discusses the importance of role allocation, emphasizing how business amateurs can identify individual strengths, promote collaboration, and create synergies within teams.

- Communication and Trust: Effective communication is the lifeblood of successful teams. This subsection explores communication strategies that build trust, foster open dialogue, and ensure that information flows seamlessly within the team, fostering a culture of transparency and collaboration.

Leadership in Team Environments:

Leadership within a team context requires a nuanced approach that balances authorlty, collaboration, and facilitation. This subsection explores the principles of team leadership, providing business amateurs with insights into leading teams to achieve their full potential.

- Servant Leadership: In team environments, leaders often serve as facilitators. This subsection introduces the concept of servant leadership, where leaders prioritize the well-being and development of team members, fostering a collaborative and empowering culture.

- Facilitating Collaboration: Effective team leaders excel at facilitating collaboration. This subsection discusses strategies for creating an environment where team members collaborate seamlessly, share ideas, and contribute to collective problem-solving.

- Conflict Resolution: Conflict is inevitable in team settings, but effective leaders know how to navigate and resolve conflicts constructively. This subsection provides business amateurs with conflict resolution strategies, emphasizing the importance of addressing conflicts promptly and fostering a positive team dynamic.

Team Building Strategies:

Successful teams are not built by chance; they are crafted through intentional team-building strategies. This subsection explores practical approaches to team building, guiding business amateurs in creating cohesive teams that are resilient, adaptive, and aligned with organizational objectives.

- Team Building Activities: Engaging team-building activities play a crucial role in fostering camaraderie and trust. This subsection provides a repertoire of team-building activities, from icebreakers to problem-solving exercises, designed to strengthen interpersonal relationships within teams.

- Diversity and Inclusion in Teams: Embracing diversity and fostering inclusion are not just moral imperatives but strategic advantages. This subsection explores how business amateurs can promote diversity and inclusion within teams, leveraging the unique strengths and perspectives that diverse teams bring.

- Team Recognition and Rewards: Recognizing and rewarding team achievements is essential for morale and motivation. This subsection discusses effective strategies for acknowledging team contributions, whether through public recognition, incentives, or team-based rewards.

4.3 Strategic Leadership and Decision-Making

Strategic leadership is the compass that guides organizations through the complexities of the business landscape. Section 4.3 unfolds as a comprehensive exploration of strategic leadership and decision-making, equipping business amateurs with the skills needed to navigate uncertainties, make informed choices, and lead organizations toward sustained success.

Visionary Leadership:

At the core of strategic leadership is visionary thinking. This subsection explores the principles of visionary leadership, emphasizing the importance of aligning organizational strategies with a compelling vision that inspires and guides teams toward a shared future.

- Crafting a Compelling Vision: Visionary leaders articulate a clear and inspiring vision for the future. This subsection provides business amateurs with practical steps for crafting a compelling vision that resonates with stakeholders and motivates teams.

- Communicating the Vision: A vision is only effective when communicated effectively. This subsection discusses communication strategies that ensure the vision is understood, embraced, and becomes a driving force for organizational alignment.

 Strategic Decision-Making Frameworks:

Strategic decision-making is a complex process that requires thoughtful analysis and a systematic approach. This subsection introduces business amateurs to strategic decision-making frameworks, providing a toolkit for evaluating options, mitigating risks, and making choices that align with organizational goals.

- SWOT Analysis Revisited: SWOT analysis is a versatile tool in strategic decision-making. This subsection revisits SWOT analysis, showcasing how business amateurs can use this framework to assess internal strengths and weaknesses, as well as external opportunities and threats.

- Cost-Benefit Analysis: Evaluating the costs and benefits of strategic decisions is paramount. This subsection introduces cost-benefit analysis as a decision-making tool, offering insights into how organizations can assess the financial implications of different choices.

- Scenario Planning for Uncertainties: The business landscape is rife with uncertainties. This subsection explores scenario planning as a strategic decision-making approach, guiding business amateurs in preparing for and mitigating the impact of potential future scenarios.

 Aligning Strategy with Organizational Goals:

Strategic leadership is about aligning the trajectory of an organization with its overarching goals. This subsection discusses the importance of aligning strategy with organizational goals, ensuring that every decision contributes to the long-term success and sustainability of the business.

- Defining Organizational Goals: Clear organizational goals provide a roadmap for strategic decision-making. This subsection delves into the process of defining and refining organizational goals, from short-term objectives to long-term aspirations.

- Strategic Initiatives and Action Plans: Goals are achieved through strategic initiatives. This subsection explores how business amateurs can develop actionable strategic initiatives and associated action plans, ensuring that organizational goals are translated into tangible steps.

Leading Change and Innovation:

In the dynamic business landscape, change and innovation are imperatives for organizational survival and growth. This subsection explores the principles of leading change and fostering innovation, providing business amateurs with the tools to drive organizational evolution.

- Change Leadership Strategies: Change often faces resistance, and effective leaders know how to navigate it. This subsection discusses change leadership strategies, emphasizing the importance of communication, engagement, and creating a culture that embraces change.

- Encouraging a Culture of Innovation: Innovation is the engine that propels organizations forward. This subsection provides insights into creating a culture that encourages innovation, from fostering creativity to implementing processes that support continuous ideation.

Ethical Considerations in Leadership:

Ethical leadership is non-negotiable in strategic leadership. This subsection explores the ethical considerations that guide strategic leaders, emphasizing the importance of integrity, transparency, and a commitment to ethical decision-making.

- Ethical Decision-Making in Strategy: Strategic decisions often come with ethical considerations. This subsection provides business amateurs with a framework for ethical decision-making in strategic contexts, ensuring that choices align with organizational values.

- Corporate Social Responsibility (CSR) in Strategy: Integrating CSR into strategic decisions is a hallmark of ethical leadership. This subsection explores how business amateurs can incorporate CSR principles into their strategic leadership approach, contributing to positive social impact.

Building effective teams and exercising strategic leadership are not just skills; they are art forms that require continuous refinement and adaptation.

With this knowledge in hand, business amateurs are poised to not only navigate but also shape the leadership landscape. From fostering teamwork and collaboration to making strategic decisions that propel organizations toward success, these sections lay the groundwork for leadership mastery—an essential element in the arsenal of the aspiring business professional. As we proceed, the business amateur emerges not just as a leader in training but as a strategic navigator, capable of steering organizations toward greatness.

Chapter Five
Navigating Challenges

Introduction:

In the unpredictable landscape of business, challenges are inevitable. Chapter Five serves as a compass for business amateurs, offering insights and strategies to navigate through common pitfalls, overcome obstacles with resilience, and draw valuable lessons from the experiences of others. As business ventures evolve, understanding and addressing challenges become paramount for sustained growth and success.

5.1 Common Pitfalls for Business Amateurs

Success in the business realm is often accompanied by a series of challenges and potential pitfalls. Section 5.1 is dedicated to illuminating these common pitfalls, providing business amateurs with a roadmap to recognize, navigate, and mitigate risks that may hinder their entrepreneurial journey.

Lack of Market Research and Understanding:

One of the primary pitfalls for business amateurs is diving into the market without thorough research and understanding. This subsection explores the consequences of inadequate market research, emphasizing the importance of knowing the target audience, understanding competitors, and staying informed about industry trends.

- The Importance of Market Research: Market research is the foundation of a successful business. This subsection delves into the methodologies of effective market research, from surveys and interviews to data analysis, empowering business amateurs to make informed decisions.

- Understanding Consumer Needs: Meeting consumer needs is the essence of business success. This subsection discusses strategies for understanding and addressing consumer needs, ensuring that products or services align with market demands.

- Competitor Analysis: Ignoring competitors can lead to missed opportunities. This subsection guides business amateurs in conducting comprehensive competitor analysis, identifying strengths and weaknesses, and leveraging insights for strategic positioning.

Inadequate Financial Planning and Management:

Financial mismanagement is a pitfall that can cripple even the most promising ventures. This subsection explores the importance of robust financial planning and management, offering business amateurs tools and strategies to navigate budgeting, cash flow, and fiscal responsibility.

- Creating a Financial Plan: A solid financial plan is the backbone of business stability. This subsection provides a step-by-step guide to creating a comprehensive financial plan, covering aspects such as budgeting, forecasting, and managing expenses.

- Cash Flow Management: Managing cash flow is critical for operational continuity. This subsection discusses strategies for effective cash flow management, including invoicing practices, payment terms, and contingency planning.

- Contingency Planning: Anticipating financial uncertainties is key. This subsection introduces the concept of contingency planning, helping business amateurs develop strategies to navigate unexpected financial challenges.

Insufficient Marketing and Branding:

In a competitive business landscape, visibility is crucial. This subsection explores the pitfalls associated with insufficient marketing and branding efforts, guiding business amateurs in creating effective strategies to build brand awareness and reach their target audience.

- The Power of Marketing: Marketing is more than promotion; it's about building relationships. This subsection explores diverse marketing channels, from digital marketing and social media to traditional advertising, helping business amateurs develop a comprehensive marketing strategy.

- Building a Strong Brand: A strong brand is a competitive advantage. This subsection provides insights into brand-building strategies, including consistent messaging, visual identity, and the cultivation of a unique brand personality.

- Digital Presence: In the digital age, an online presence is non-negotiable. This subsection discusses the importance of a robust digital presence, offering guidance on website development, SEO, and leveraging digital platforms for marketing.

Poor Leadership and Team Management:

The effectiveness of leadership and team management significantly influences organizational success. This subsection explores the pitfalls associated with poor leadership and provides business amateurs with guidance on cultivating strong leadership skills and fostering a positive team dynamic.

- Leadership Styles: Effective leadership comes in various styles. This subsection discusses different leadership styles, from transformational and servant leadership to situational leadership, empowering business amateurs to identify and adopt styles that align with their organizational culture.

- Team Building: A cohesive team is a valuable asset. This subsection delves into strategies for team building, from effective communication and conflict resolution to recognizing and leveraging individual strengths within the team.

- Cultivating a Positive Work Culture: A positive work culture is essential for employee satisfaction and productivity. This subsection provides insights into fostering a positive work environment, emphasizing the importance of employee well-being, recognition, and a shared sense of purpose.

Inadequate Adaptability and Innovation:

In a rapidly changing business landscape, adaptability and innovation are prerequisites for success. This subsection explores the pitfalls associated with resistance to change and a lack of innovation, guiding business amateurs in cultivating a mindset that embraces evolution.

- Embracing Change: Change is constant; successful businesses adapt. This subsection discusses the importance of change management, offering strategies for embracing change, fostering a culture of adaptability, and navigating uncertainties.

- Encouraging Innovation: Innovation is a catalyst for growth. This subsection provides insights into creating an innovative culture, from encouraging creativity and experimentation to implementing processes that support continuous improvement.

- Staying Ahead of Trends: Anticipating trends is a strategic advantage. This subsection explores methods for staying informed about industry trends, technological advancements, and market shifts, enabling business amateurs to position themselves ahead of the curve.

Section 5.1 serves as a comprehensive guide, shedding light on common pitfalls that business amateurs may encounter. By addressing these challenges proactively, business professionals can fortify their ventures, laying the groundwork for sustained growth and success. As we delve into Section 5.2, the focus shifts to strategies for overcoming obstacles with resilience, equipping business amateurs with the tools needed to navigate adversity and emerge stronger on the other side.

5.2 Overcoming Obstacles with Resilience
In the intricate dance of entrepreneurship, obstacles are not roadblocks but rather stepping stones to growth. Section 5.2 delves into the art of overcoming challenges with resilience, providing business amateurs with the mindset and strategies needed to navigate adversity and emerge stronger on their entrepreneurial journey.

Resilience Mindset:

Embracing Challenges as Opportunities:

Resilience begins with a mindset that views challenges not as insurmountable obstacles but as opportunities for growth and learning. This subsection explores the concept of a resilience mindset, encouraging business amateurs to shift their perspective and view challenges as integral parts of the entrepreneurial journey.

- Cultivating a Growth Mindset: A growth mindset is foundational to resilience. This subsection discusses the principles of a growth mindset, emphasizing the importance of continuous learning, adaptability, and the belief that abilities can be developed over time.

- Learning from Setbacks: Every setback is a lesson. This subsection guides business amateurs in extracting valuable insights from challenges, using setbacks as opportunities to refine strategies, improve processes, and enhance overall business resilience.

- Developing Emotional Intelligence: Emotional intelligence is a cornerstone of resilience. This subsection explores the role of emotional intelligence in navigating challenges, offering strategies for self-awareness, self-regulation, and effective interpersonal relationships.

Strategies for Overcoming Business Challenges:

Adaptive Leadership:

In the face of challenges, leadership is not about avoiding difficulties but about navigating them adeptly. This subsection explores adaptive leadership, providing insights into strategies that enable business amateurs to lead effectively in dynamic and uncertain environments.

- Agile Decision-Making: Agile decision-making is crucial in dynamic settings. This subsection discusses principles of agile decision-making, empowering business amateurs to make informed choices promptly, adjust strategies as needed, and navigate uncertainties with confidence.

- Leading by Example: Leadership is most influential when demonstrated. This subsection emphasizes the importance of leading by example, showcasing resilience, adaptability, and a positive mindset as essential qualities that inspire and motivate teams.

- Building a Resilient Team Culture: Resilience is not an individual endeavor; it thrives in a resilient team culture. This subsection provides guidance on fostering a culture of resilience within teams, promoting collaboration, open communication, and mutual support.

Financial Resilience:

Financial challenges are inherent in business, and building financial resilience is key to weathering economic uncertainties. This subsection explores strategies for financial resilience, from prudent financial planning to creating contingency funds that act as buffers during tough times.

- Scenario Planning for Financial Stability: Scenario planning is a proactive approach to financial resilience. This subsection guides business amateurs in creating financial scenarios, identifying potential challenges, and developing strategies to mitigate financial risks.

- Diversification of Revenue Streams: Relying on a single revenue stream can be precarious. This subsection discusses the importance of diversifying revenue streams, exploring new markets, and offering complementary products or services to enhance financial stability.

- Building Strong Vendor Relationships: Vendor relationships are integral to business operations. This subsection explores strategies for building strong vendor relationships, emphasizing communication, mutual understanding, and collaborative problem-solving to ensure a resilient supply chain.

Leveraging Technology for Resilience:

Technology is a powerful ally in building business resilience. This subsection explores how business amateurs can leverage technology to not only navigate challenges but also drive innovation and enhance overall business efficiency.

- Digital Transformation Strategies: Digital transformation is more than a buzzword; it's a resilience strategy. This subsection provides insights into digital transformation strategies, from adopting cloud technologies to automating processes, enabling businesses to adapt swiftly to changing environments.

- Data-Driven Decision-Making: Informed decisions are resilient decisions. This subsection discusses the role of data-driven decision-making, guiding business amateurs in collecting and analyzing data to gain insights that inform strategic choices.

- Cybersecurity for Business Continuity: As businesses embrace technology, cybersecurity becomes paramount. This subsection explores cybersecurity measures that business amateurs can implement to protect their operations, customer data, and overall business continuity.

Emotional Resilience and Well-being:

Managing Stress and Burnout:

The entrepreneurial journey can be demanding, leading to stress and burnout. This subsection explores strategies for managing stress, promoting mental well-being, and cultivating a resilient mindset that enables business amateurs to navigate challenges without compromising their health.

- Stress Management Techniques: This subsection discusses practical stress management techniques, from mindfulness practices to time management strategies, empowering business professionals to maintain balance and resilience amid demanding workloads.

- Recognizing and Addressing Burnout: Burnout is a real threat to entrepreneurial well-being. This subsection provides insights into recognizing burnout symptoms, fostering a culture that encourages open discussions about mental health, and seeking professional support when needed.

- Work-Life Integration: Striking a balance between work and personal life is essential for sustained resilience. This subsection explores the concept of work-life integration, encouraging business amateurs to create boundaries, prioritize self-care, and nurture a holistic approach to well-being.

Case Studies: Learning from Others' Experiences

Real-Life Lessons in Resilience:

Learning from the experiences of others is a powerful way to cultivate resilience. This subsection presents case studies of businesses that faced significant challenges, highlighting the strategies they employed to overcome adversity and emerge stronger.

- Adapting to Market Shifts: Case studies illustrate how businesses navigated market shifts, adapted their strategies, and leveraged opportunities arising from changes in consumer behavior or industry trends.

- Financial Turnarounds: Examining cases of businesses that experienced financial challenges provides valuable insights into the strategies they employed to achieve financial resilience and stability.

- Leadership in Crisis: Real-life stories of leadership during crises showcase the qualities and strategies that effective leaders employed to steer their organizations through tumultuous times.

Section 5.2 dives into the art of overcoming obstacles with resilience, offering business amateurs a comprehensive guide to navigating challenges with a positive mindset and effective strategies. By embracing challenges as opportunities for growth, adapting leadership approaches, building financial and technological resilience, and prioritizing emotional well-being, business professionals can not only navigate adversity but also thrive amid uncertainty. As we transition to Section 5.3, the focus turns to case studies, providing real-life lessons that illuminate the principles of resilience in action.

Case Studies: Learning from Others' Experiences
Learning from real-world experiences is a potent tool for business amateurs seeking to navigate challenges and cultivate resilience. Section 5.3 delves into case studies, offering a close examination of businesses that faced significant obstacles, the strategies they employed, and the lessons that can be gleaned from their experiences. These narratives serve as invaluable lessons, providing insights and inspiration for business professionals on their own entrepreneurial journey.

Case Study 1: Adapting to Market Shifts

Background:

In the dynamic landscape of business, market shifts are inevitable. This case study explores a business that adeptly navigated a substantial market shift, demonstrating resilience in the face of change.

Key Learnings:

- Agile Business Models: The business's ability to swiftly adjust its business model showcased the importance of agility. Business amateurs can learn to assess market dynamics, identify signs of change, and proactively adapt their strategies.

- Customer-Centric Approach: This case study emphasizes the significance of a customer-centric approach. The business prioritized understanding its customers' evolving needs, allowing it to tailor products and services to align with shifting market demands.

- Innovation as a Response: Rather than resisting change, the business embraced innovation. This case study illustrates how embracing new technologies and creative solutions enabled the

business to stay ahead of the curve and thrive in the evolving market.
Case Study 2: Financial Turnarounds

Background:

Financial challenges can be formidable, but this case study explores a business that successfully navigated a financial turnaround, providing valuable insights into strategies for fiscal resilience.

Key Learnings:

- Rigorous Financial Planning: The business implemented rigorous financial planning, emphasizing the importance of creating detailed budgets, forecasting effectively, and regularly assessing financial health. Business amateurs can adopt similar financial planning practices to fortify their ventures.

- Cost-Efficiency Measures: This case study delves into the cost-efficiency measures employed by the business. Learning to identify and implement cost-saving strategies can be instrumental for businesses facing financial challenges.

- Negotiation and Collaboration: Negotiating with stakeholders and fostering collaborative relationships played a pivotal role in the financial turnaround. Business professionals can learn to navigate negotiations effectively and leverage collaborations to achieve financial stability.

Case Study 3: Leadership in Crisis

Background:

Effective leadership during crises is a testament to resilience. This case study explores a business that demonstrated strong leadership amidst a crisis, providing insights into qualities and strategies that proved instrumental.

Key Learnings:

- Transparent Communication: Transparent communication emerged as a cornerstone of effective leadership. This case study highlights the importance of leaders being open and honest with their teams, fostering trust and unity during challenging times.

- Decisive Decision-Making: In times of crisis, decisive decision-making is imperative. This case study illustrates how the business leader made timely and well-informed decisions, showcasing the importance of decisiveness in leadership.

- Employee Support Initiatives: Supporting employees during crises is a hallmark of effective leadership. The case study explores initiatives implemented by the business to prioritize employee well-being, offering valuable lessons for leaders seeking to nurture a resilient team culture.

Conclusion of Section 5.3:

Case studies provide a rich tapestry of real-world experiences, offering business amateurs a front-row seat to the challenges, strategies, and outcomes of businesses facing adversity. As we conclude Section 5.3, the overarching lesson is that resilience is not only about weathering storms but also about adapting, innovating, and leading with fortitude. By immersing themselves in these case studies, business professionals can draw inspiration and practical insights, forging a path of resilience in their own entrepreneurial endeavors. The journey of learning from others' experiences continues to be an invaluable resource on the road to success.

Chapter Six:
Financial Literacy for Business Amateurs

Introduction:

Financial literacy is the bedrock of sound business management. Chapter Six aims to demystify the complexities of finance for business amateurs, providing a comprehensive guide to understanding financial statements, mastering budgeting and financial planning, and formulating effective financial strategies for success. In the intricate dance of business, financial acumen is a vital skill that empowers entrepreneurs to make informed decisions, navigate economic uncertainties, and drive sustained growth.

6.1 Understanding Financial Statements

Introduction:

Financial statements are the heartbeat of a business, offering a snapshot of its financial health. Section 6.1 delves into the fundamentals of financial statements, empowering business amateurs to decipher balance sheets, income statements, and cash flow statements with confidence.

The Balance Sheet:

Assets, Liabilities, and Equity:

Understanding the balance sheet is akin to reading a business's financial story. This subsection breaks down the components of a balance sheet, from assets and liabilities to equity. Business amateurs will gain insights into how these elements interplay to reflect the company's financial position.

- Assets: The assets section encompasses what the business owns. This subsection explores current and noncurrent assets, providing clarity on their classification and significance in assessing liquidity and long-term value.

- Liabilities: Liabilities represent the company's obligations. Business amateurs will learn to distinguish between current and long-term liabilities, understanding their impact on the business's financial obligations and solvency.

- Equity: Equity is the residual interest in the assets after deducting liabilities. This subsection elucidates the concept of equity, offering insights into the ownership structure and the relationship between equity and a company's net worth.

The Income Statement:

Revenue, Expenses, and Profitability:

The income statement narrates a business's financial performance over a specific period. This subsection dissects the income statement, unraveling revenue streams, various expenses, and the crucial metric of profitability.

- Revenue Streams: Understanding how a business generates revenue is foundational. Business amateurs will explore different revenue streams, recognizing the primary sources that contribute to the top line.

- Operating Expenses: Every business incurs operating expenses. This subsection delineates common operating expenses, providing insights into cost structures and how they impact the bottom line.

- Profitability Ratios: Profitability is the litmus test of a business's success. Business amateurs will delve into key profitability ratios, including gross profit margin, operating profit margin, and net profit margin, gaining a nuanced understanding of financial performance.

The Cash Flow Statement:

Operating, Investing, and Financing Activities:

Cash is the lifeblood of a business, and the cash flow statement tracks its inflows and outflows. This subsection deciphers the cash flow statement, shedding light on operating, investing, and financing activities.

- Operating Activities: Operating cash flow reflects a business's core operations. Business amateurs will learn to analyze cash generated or consumed by day-to-day activities, gauging the company's ability to sustain its operations.

- Investing Activities: Investments shape a business's future. This subsection explores cash flows related to investments in assets, providing insights into how capital expenditures and asset acquisitions impact overall financial health.

- Financing Activities: How a business raises capital is crucial. Business amateurs will understand cash flows from financing activities, encompassing debt, equity, and dividend transactions, offering a holistic view of a company's financial structure.

Financial Statement Analysis:

Ratios, Trends, and Benchmarks:

Financial statements become actionable insights through analysis. This subsection equips business amateurs with tools to conduct financial statement analysis, from key financial ratios to identifying trends and benchmarking against industry standards.

- Liquidity Ratios: Liquidity is vital for operational resilience. Business amateurs will explore liquidity ratios such as the current ratio and quick ratio, understanding how these metrics assess a company's ability to meet short-term obligations.

- Profitability Analysis: Profitability is multifaceted. This subsection introduces business amateurs to advanced profitability analysis, including return on assets (ROA) and return on equity (ROE), offering nuanced perspectives on a company's financial efficiency.

- Financial Trends: Trends unveil a business's trajectory. Business amateurs will learn to identify financial trends, differentiating between short-term fluctuations and long-term shifts that can impact strategic decision-making.

- Industry Benchmarks: Context is crucial in financial analysis. This subsection emphasizes the importance of benchmarking against industry standards, empowering business amateurs to assess performance relative to peers and identify areas for improvement.

Armed with this knowledge, entrepreneurs can decipher the financial narratives of their ventures, make informed decisions, and establish a solid foundation for financial success. As we transition to Section 6.2, the focus turns to budgeting and financial planning, essential elements in the arsenal of business professionals seeking to steer their ventures toward prosperity.

6.2 Budgeting and Financial Planning

Budgeting and financial planning are the architects of a stable and thriving business. Section 6.2 delves into the art and science of budgeting, guiding business amateurs in crafting robust financial plans that align with strategic goals, allocate resources efficiently, and pave the way for sustainable growth.

The Significance of Budgeting:

Strategic Allocation of Resources:

Budgets are more than financial roadmaps; they are strategic tools for resource allocation. This subsection explores the significance of budgeting in aligning financial resources with business priorities and goals.

- Strategic Goal Alignment: Business amateurs will learn to translate strategic goals into budgetary allocations, ensuring that financial resources are directed toward initiatives that drive growth, innovation, and overall success.

- Resource Efficiency: Budgets enable efficient resource utilization. This subsection discusses how budgeting helps businesses avoid resource wastage, allocate funds judiciously, and optimize the use of financial resources.

- Flexibility and Adaptability: In a dynamic business environment, flexibility is key. Business amateurs will explore the importance of creating flexible budgets that can adapt to changing circumstances, fostering agility in financial planning.

Components of a Comprehensive Budget:

Revenue, Operating Expenses, and Capital Expenditures:

Crafting a comprehensive budget involves meticulous consideration of revenue streams, operating expenses, and capital expenditures. This subsection provides a detailed examination of these components, offering practical insights for effective budget formulation.

- Revenue Projections: Accurate revenue projections are foundational to budgeting. Business amateurs will learn methodologies for forecasting revenues, incorporating market trends, customer behavior, and other factors into their projections.

- Operating Expense Budgets: Operating expenses are the backbone of a budget. This subsection guides business amateurs in creating detailed operating expense budgets, categorizing expenses, and identifying opportunities for cost optimization.

- Capital Expenditure Planning: Capital expenditures shape a business's future. Business amateurs will explore strategies for planning and budgeting capital expenditures, aligning investment decisions with long-term strategic objectives.

Budget Monitoring and Control:

Metrics, Variance Analysis, and Decision-Making:

A budget is not a static document; it requires vigilant monitoring and control. This subsection delves into key metrics, variance analysis, and decision-making processes that empower business amateurs to keep their budgets on track.

- Key Performance Indicators (KPIs): Effective budget monitoring relies on relevant KPIs. Business amateurs will learn to identify and track KPIs that provide insights into financial performance, enabling proactive decision-making.

- Variance Analysis: Variances are inevitable, but understanding them is crucial. This subsection introduces variance analysis, helping business professionals interpret discrepancies between budgeted and actual figures and take corrective actions.

- Adaptive Decision-Making: Budgets inform decision-making. Business amateurs will explore how adaptive decision-making, informed by budgetary insights, enables them to respond swiftly to opportunities, challenges, and changes in the business environment.

Financial Planning for Growth:

Forecasting, Scenario Planning, and Strategic Initiatives:

Financial planning extends beyond budgets; it encompasses forecasting, scenario planning, and strategic initiatives that position a business for sustained growth. This subsection explores these elements, providing a holistic view of financial planning.

- Financial Forecasting: Forecasting is the compass for the future. Business amateurs will learn to create financial forecasts that project future financial performance, aiding in long-term planning and strategic decision-making.

- Scenario Planning: Uncertainties are part of business. This subsection introduces scenario planning, allowing business professionals to prepare for various future scenarios, identify potential challenges, and formulate strategies to navigate uncertainties.

- Strategic Financial Initiatives: Financial planning drives strategic initiatives. Business amateurs will explore how financial planning aligns with strategic goals, facilitating the implementation of initiatives that propel the business forward.

6.3 Financial Strategies for Success

Financial success is the culmination of strategic decisions, prudent management, and a proactive approach to navigating the complexities of the business landscape. Section 6.3 delves into advanced financial strategies, providing business amateurs with a toolkit to optimize financial performance, mitigate risks, and position their ventures for sustained success.

Optimal Capital Structure:

Balancing Debt and Equity:

The composition of a business's capital structure plays a pivotal role in its financial health. This subsection explores the nuances of optimizing the capital structure, striking a balance between debt and equity to enhance overall financial stability.

- Debt Financing Strategies: Debt can be a powerful catalyst for growth. Business amateurs will learn strategies for leveraging debt, understanding different types of debt instruments, and managing debt to optimize financial leverage.

- Equity Financing Considerations: Equity is the foundation of ownership. This subsection discusses considerations for equity financing, including the issuance of stocks, dividends, and equity dilution, empowering business professionals to make informed decisions about their capital mix.

- Risk Management in Capital Structure: The capital structure impacts risk. Business amateurs will explore risk management strategies associated with different capital structures, ensuring that the chosen mix aligns with the business's risk tolerance and strategic objectives.

Working Capital Management:

Efficiency in Short-Term Assets and Liabilities:

Effective working capital management is the heartbeat of operational efficiency. This subsection provides insights into optimizing short-term assets and liabilities, ensuring that businesses maintain a healthy cash flow and meet day-to-day operational needs.

- Cash Conversion Cycle Optimization: The cash conversion cycle is a key metric. Business amateurs will learn to optimize this cycle, minimizing the time it takes to convert raw materials into cash, thereby enhancing liquidity and working capital efficiency.

- Inventory Management Strategies: Inventory can be a double-edged sword. This subsection explores inventory management strategies, including just-in-time (JIT) inventory systems and ABC analysis, enabling businesses to strike a balance between inventory levels and demand.

- Accounts Receivable and Payable Management: Balancing receivables and payables is critical. Business professionals will gain insights into managing accounts receivable to accelerate cash inflows and negotiating favorable payment terms with suppliers to optimize cash outflows.

Financial Risk Mitigation:

Hedging, Insurance, and Derivatives:

Financial risks are inherent in business, but strategic measures can mitigate their impact. This subsection delves into financial risk mitigation strategies, including hedging, insurance, and the use of derivatives to safeguard businesses against market uncertainties.

- Currency and Interest Rate Hedging: Global businesses face currency and interest rate risks. This subsection explores hedging strategies to protect against fluctuations in exchange rates and interest rates, ensuring financial stability in the face of market volatility.

- Insurance for Business Risks: Insurance is a risk transfer mechanism. Business amateurs will learn to assess different types of insurance, from property and liability insurance to business interruption coverage, tailoring insurance strategies to mitigate specific business risks.

- Derivative Instruments: Derivatives can be used strategically. This subsection introduces derivative instruments such as futures and options, illustrating how businesses can use them to manage risks associated with commodities, interest rates, and other financial variables.

Profitability Enhancement Strategies:

Margins, Pricing, and Cost Optimization:

Enhancing profitability is a multifaceted endeavor. This subsection explores advanced strategies for improving profit margins, optimizing pricing strategies, and streamlining costs to boost overall financial performance.

- Gross and Net Profit Margin Enhancement: Profit margins are key indicators of financial health. Business amateurs will learn strategies to enhance both gross and net profit margins, including cost of goods sold (COGS) optimization and revenue diversification.

- Strategic Pricing Models: Pricing is a strategic lever. This subsection discusses advanced pricing models, including value-based pricing and dynamic pricing, empowering businesses to set prices that reflect the perceived value of their products or services.

- Cost Optimization Techniques: Operational efficiency is tied to cost optimization. Business professionals will explore techniques for streamlining costs, from process reengineering and technology adoption to strategic sourcing and supply chain optimization.

Sustainable Growth Financing:

Balancing Growth and Financial Stability:

Sustainable growth requires a delicate balance between expansion and financial stability. This subsection explores financing strategies that support long-term growth while safeguarding the financial health of the business.

- Retained Earnings and Internal Financing: Retained earnings are a powerful internal financing source. Business amateurs will learn how to harness retained earnings for growth initiatives, striking a balance between internal financing and external capital.

- Venture Capital and Private Equity: External financing avenues exist for growth. This subsection provides insights into venture capital and private equity funding, guiding businesses in navigating these sources of external capital while considering implications for ownership and strategic alignment.

- Debt Financing for Growth: Debt can fuel growth if managed wisely. This subsection explores debt financing strategies for expansion, including considerations for long-term and short-term debt, interest rates, and debt covenants.

Chapter Seven
Building a Personal Brand

Introduction:

In a world marked by connectivity and constant communication, building a personal brand is a strategic imperative for business professionals. Chapter Seven explores the importance of personal branding, offering insights and practical strategies for business amateurs to craft a compelling personal brand that resonates with their target audience, establishes credibility, and opens doors to new opportunities.

7.1 The Importance of Personal Branding:

Differentiation, Credibility, and Networking:

Personal branding is more than self-promotion; it's a strategic tool for differentiation, establishing credibility, and expanding professional networks. This subsection unpacks the significance of personal branding in the context of modern business dynamics.

- Differentiation in a Crowded Market: Business professionals will learn how personal branding sets them apart in a competitive market, helping them stand out and be recognized for their unique qualities, expertise, and value proposition.

- Credibility and Trust Building: Personal branding is a trust-building exercise. This subsection explores how a strong personal brand instills confidence in others, fostering trust and credibility that can be instrumental in business interactions and collaborations.

- Networking and Relationship Building: Networking is a cornerstone of success. Business amateurs will gain insights into how personal branding enhances networking efforts, opening doors to new opportunities, partnerships, and collaborations.

7.2 Developing Your Professional Image:

Authenticity, Consistency, and Online Presence:

Crafting a professional image requires authenticity, consistency, and a strategic online presence. This subsection provides guidance on building and maintaining a professional image that aligns with personal values and resonates with the intended audience.

- Authenticity in Personal Branding: Authenticity is magnetic. Business professionals will learn to embrace authenticity in their personal branding efforts, showcasing their true selves to build genuine connections with their audience.

- Consistency Across Platforms: In a digital age, consistency is key. This subsection explores the importance of maintaining a consistent brand image across various platforms, from social media profiles to professional networks, reinforcing brand recognition.

- Strategic Online Presence: The internet is a powerful personal branding tool. Business amateurs will gain practical tips on cultivating a strategic online presence, optimizing social media profiles, and leveraging digital platforms to enhance their visibility and influence.

7.3 Leveraging Social Media and Networking:

Platforms, Engagement, and Thought Leadership:

Social media is a dynamic landscape for personal branding, and strategic networking enhances brand reach. This subsection delves into the nuances of leveraging social media and networking for effective personal branding.

- Choosing the Right Platforms: Not all social media platforms are created equal. Business professionals will learn to identify the platforms that align with their personal brand, target audience, and communication style, optimizing their presence for maximum impact.

- Engagement Strategies: Engagement builds relationships. This subsection provides insights into effective engagement strategies on social media, encouraging business amateurs to interact, share insights, and contribute meaningfully to online conversations.
- Becoming a Thought Leader: Thought leadership commands attention. Business professionals will explore strategies for becoming a thought leader in their industry, positioning themselves as authorities and influencers through the creation and sharing of valuable content.

Chapter Eight
Resources and Tools for Business Amateurs

Introduction:

Continuous learning and professional development are essential for business amateurs navigating the ever-evolving landscape of entrepreneurship. Chapter Eight compiles a curated set of resources and tools, offering business professionals valuable insights, in-depth knowledge, and practical skills to enhance their capabilities and drive success in their ventures.

8.1 Recommended Books and Reading:

Knowledge Enrichment and Insightful Perspectives:

Books are a timeless source of knowledge and wisdom. This subsection presents a carefully curated list of recommended books and reading materials covering a spectrum of topics relevant to business amateurs, from entrepreneurship and leadership to finance and personal development.

- Entrepreneurship Classics: Explore timeless works by entrepreneurial thought leaders, gaining insights into the mindset, strategies, and challenges of successful entrepreneurs.

- Leadership and Management: Delve into books on leadership and management, learning from experienced leaders and discovering effective strategies for leading teams and organizations.

- Finance and Business Strategy: Enhance financial acumen and strategic thinking with books that demystify finance, illuminate business strategy, and offer practical insights for success.

- Personal Development and Growth: Personal development is integral to professional success. This subsection recommends books that inspire personal growth, resilience, and a holistic approach to life and business.

8.2 Online Courses and Learning Platforms:

Skill Enhancement and Specialized Knowledge:

In the digital age, online courses are powerful tools for skill enhancement and knowledge acquisition. This subsection introduces a curated selection of online courses and learning platforms tailored for business amateurs, covering a diverse range of subjects.

- Entrepreneurship Courses: Immerse yourself in courses that provide a comprehensive understanding of entrepreneurship, from idea generation and business planning to execution and growth.
- Leadership and Management Programs: Sharpen your leadership and management skills through

online programs that offer practical frameworks, case studies, and interactive learning experiences.
- Financial Literacy Training: Gain financial acumen through online courses that demystify financial statements, budgeting, and strategic financial management.

- Digital Marketing and Branding: Explore courses on digital marketing and branding, acquiring skills to leverage online platforms, build a strong digital presence, and enhance your personal brand.

8.3 Networking Events and Communities:

Connection Building and Collaborative Learning:

Networking is a cornerstone of professional growth. This subsection highlights networking events and communities where business amateurs can connect with peers, industry experts, and mentors, fostering collaboration, learning, and opportunities.

- Industry Conferences: Attend industry-specific conferences to stay abreast of trends, connect with professionals in your field, and gain insights from keynote speakers and panel discussions.

- Online Networking Platforms: Explore online networking platforms that facilitate virtual connections, allowing business professionals to engage with a global community and expand their network.

- Professional Associations: Joining professional associations provides access to exclusive events, resources, and a network of like-minded Chapter Nine: Moving Forward - Crafting Your Business Journey

Chapter Nine
Moving Forward: Crafting Your Business Journey

Introduction:

Crafting a personalized business journey is a dynamic and empowering process. Chapter Nine guides business amateurs in setting meaningful goals, creating actionable plans, and embracing the spirit of continuous learning. This chapter serves as a roadmap for navigating challenges, seizing opportunities, and achieving milestones on the path to entrepreneurial success.

9.1 Setting Goals and Milestones:

Clarity, Specificity, and Alignment:

Setting clear and specific goals is the foundation of a purpose-driven business journey. This subsection explores the principles of goal-setting, emphasizing the importance of clarity, specificity, and alignment with personal and professional values.

- Defining Long-Term Objectives: Business amateurs will learn to articulate long-term objectives that reflect their vision for the future, providing a compass for strategic decision-making and resource allocation.

- Setting SMART Goals: The SMART criteria (Specific, Measurable, Achievable, Relevant, Time-bound) serve as a guide for effective goal-setting. This subsection breaks down each element, empowering entrepreneurs to craft goals that are both ambitious and attainable.

- Aligning Goals with Values: A harmonious alignment between goals and personal values enhances motivation and fulfillment. Business professionals will explore strategies for ensuring that their goals resonate with their core values and aspirations.

9.2 Creating a Personalized Action Plan:

Strategic Roadmap and Tactical Execution:

Goals are brought to life through actionable plans. This subsection delves into the process of creating a personalized action plan, combining strategic thinking with tactical execution to transform aspirations into reality.

- Breaking Down Goals into Tasks: Business amateurs will learn to deconstruct overarching goals into manageable tasks, fostering a step-by-step approach that enhances clarity and focus.

- Prioritizing and Sequencing Tasks: Effective prioritization is key to efficient execution. This subsection explores techniques for prioritizing tasks based on urgency, importance, and dependencies, enabling entrepreneurs to sequence their actions for optimal impact.

- Resource Allocation and Time Management: Strategic resource allocation, including financial, human, and time resources, is crucial for plan execution. Business professionals will gain insights into effective resource management and time allocation, maximizing efficiency.

9.3 Embracing Continuous Learning:

Curiosity, Adaptability, and Professional Growth:

The entrepreneurial journey is a continuous learning experience. This subsection emphasizes the importance of embracing a mindset of continuous learning, fostering curiosity, adaptability, and a commitment to ongoing professional growth.

- Curating a Personal Learning Path: Business amateurs will explore strategies for curating a personalized learning path, incorporating a mix of formal education, self-directed study, and experiential learning to expand their knowledge base.

- Adapting to Industry Changes: The business landscape is dynamic. Entrepreneurs will gain insights into staying abreast of industry changes, anticipating trends, and adapting their strategies to navigate evolving market conditions.

- Mentorship and Networking for Learning: Leveraging mentorship and networking opportunities enhances the learning journey. This subsection explores the benefits of connecting with mentors, industry experts, and peers to gain insights, guidance, and diverse perspectives.
As we approach the final chapter, Chapter Ten reflects on the business amateur's journey, prompting reflection, evaluation, and a forward-looking stance toward the next steps in their business endeavors.d individuals in your industry.

Chapter Ten
Conclusion

10.1 Reflecting on Your Business Amateur Journey:

Self-Discovery, Challenges, and Achievements:

As business amateurs conclude their journey, this section prompts reflection on the transformative experiences, self-discovery, challenges overcome, and achievements celebrated. Entrepreneurs are encouraged to acknowledge the growth they've undergone and the valuable lessons learned throughout the journey.

- Self-Discovery: Reflecting on personal and professional growth fosters self-awareness. Business professionals will explore how the journey has shaped their identity, values, and aspirations, setting the stage for continued personal development.

- Challenges Overcome: Every challenge is an opportunity for growth. Entrepreneurs will reflect on the challenges they faced, examining the strategies employed to overcome obstacles and the resilience developed in the process.

- Celebrating Achievements: Recognizing and celebrating achievements is essential for motivation. This subsection encourages business amateurs to acknowledge their successes, both big and small, and appreciate the milestones achieved on their entrepreneurial path.

10.2 Taking the Next Steps in Your Business Endeavors:

Future Vision, Adaptability, and Sustained Growth:

As business amateurs conclude their journey, the focus shifts to the future. This section guides entrepreneurs in envisioning the next steps in their business endeavors, fostering adaptability, and outlining strategies for sustained growth.

- Future Vision and Goals: Entrepreneurs will articulate their future vision for their business endeavors, setting new goals and aspirations that build upon the foundation laid during the business amateur journey.

- Adaptability in a Dynamic Landscape: The business landscape is ever-evolving. This subsection emphasizes the importance of adaptability, encouraging entrepreneurs to stay agile, embrace change, and adjust strategies to meet evolving market dynamics.

- Strategies for Sustained Growth: Sustainable growth requires strategic planning. Business professionals will explore advanced strategies for sustaining and accelerating growth, including diversification, innovation, and strategic partnerships.